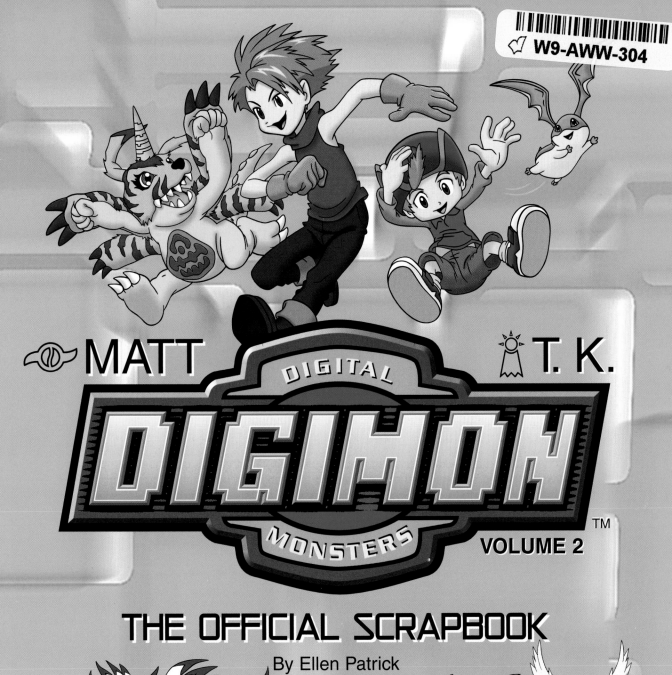

MATT   T. K.

DIGITAL DIGIMON MONSTERS

™ VOLUME 2

THE OFFICIAL SCRAPBOOK

By Ellen Patrick

SCHOLASTIC INC.

New York   Toronto   London   Auckland   Sydney
Mexico City   New Delhi   Hong Kong

ISBN 0-439-22853-0

All rights reserved. Published by Scholastic Inc.
SCHOLASTIC and associated logos are trademarks
and/or registered trademarks of Scholastic Inc.

Produced by Southern Lights Custom Publishing

12 11 10 9 8 7 6 5 4 3 2   0 1 2 3 4 5 6/0

Printed in the U.S.A.
First Scholastic printing, October 2000

HELLO, WE'RE MATT & T.K.!

Tsunomon

Gabumon

Garurumon

I'm Matt, and I've got some powerful Digimon friends on my side. I can't wait for you to meet them!

Tokomon

Patamon

Angemon

I'm T. K. My Digimons take such good care of me, I don't know where I'd be without them. Come on, and let us show you more about DigiWorld!

WE'RE BROTHERS!

We might look a little scared sometimes, but saving the world from evil Digimons gets a little scary!

Here's some stuff you need to know about us:

MATT

- I'm the older brother!

- People say I'm cool.

- I don't like to be bossed around.

- Girls like a guy like me — tough, cool, and good-looking!

- I love playing the harmonica.

- Our parents are divorced so I don't see T. K. a lot — that is, until we got to DigiWorld. I guess I have to put up with the little dude now.

T. K.

- I'm the younger brother!

- I might be little, but I'm loud!

- I'll show Matt that I can be as tough as he is. (Even if I do cry just a little sometimes.)

- I'm not sure how much I like it in DigiWorld but I'm glad Matt's with me.

- I'm really glad we have our Digimons, too!

- I don't know if Matt misses Dad, but I sure miss Mom.

HERE IS HOW DIGIWORLD!

"The sky is, like, short-circuiting!" – Matt

WE GOT TO

We were just minding our own business
at summer camp, and it started to snow.

These blinking
things fell out of
the sky and when
we picked them up
we got whooshed
here!

OUR DIGIMON
TSUNOMON 8

"Tsunomon is my name and I am quite pleased to meet you... and very loyal."
— Tsunomon

FRIENDS TOKOMON

Not long after we landed in DigiWorld, these little guys came out to meet us! Now Tsunomon is Matt's personal protector and best friend Digimon, and Tokomon is the same for T. K.

Tsunomon and Tokomon are both Micro Digimons, in what you might think of as the "infant" or "In-Training" stage for a Digimon.

In fact all our Digimons started out as Micro Digimons, who were "In-Training" when we first got to DigiWorld.

"We're Digimon, Digital Monsters!"
— The Digimons

OUR HUMAN THEIR GOOD

Five of our friends came to DigiWorld with us! Here they are, with their Digimons!

Sora & Yokomon

Tai & Koromon

Mimi & Tanemon

FRIENDS AND DIGIMONS

Izzy & Motimon

Joe & Bukamon

DIGI-KNOW?

 TAI is our leader — a very brave guy. His Digimon Koromon is tough too, but more of the deep-thinker type.

MIMI is a little bit of a princess, but we love her anyway. Her Digimon Tanemon is also on the light and fluffy side, but helps keep Mimi down to earth, believe it or not!

 SORA is the voice of reason. She really keeps an eye on us. Her Digimon Yokomon tries to get her to lighten up.

IZZY is our in house computer genius. He practically LIVES inside his computer! Motimon, his Digimon, helps keep Izzy in touch with the big picture.

JOE worries about...well, everything! His Digimon Bukamon is just what Joe needs, laid-back and ready for fun.

TSUNOMON & DIGIVOLVE!!!

 The coolest thing about our Digimons is that they can DIGIVOLVE to a higher, stronger level of fighter! After the In-Training level, they Digivolve to "Rookie"! Somehow those bright things that fell down from the sky, our "Digivices," help them Digivolve so that now, when there's danger, we have our Digimons by our side in a new, improved form!

ガブモン

GABUMON

Tsunomon Digivolves to Gabumon!

TOKOMON

パタモン
PATAMON

And Tokomon Digivolves to Patamon!

OUR DIGIMONS WEAPONS!

Blue Blaster!

Gabumon fights against evil and bad Digimons with his secret weapon of powerful blue fire that comes out of his mouth whenever Matt's in trouble! When that happens, Gabumon yells "BLUE BLASTER!!!"

HAVE SECRET

Boom Bubbles!

Patamon has his own secret weapon in the amazing BOOM BUBBLES he can blow! Patamon's BOOM BUBBLES are so powerful, he sometimes almost blows himself out of the picture just firing them off!

17

WE HAVE SECRET WEAPONS, TOO –

A DIGI-SECRET MESSAGE*
*To read, hold in front of mirror.

The earliest known sign of a Digivice is an ancient symbol on the wall of a cave on the Continent of Server.

Their Digivices sure helped Tai and Matt get the Black Gears out of Leomon.

OUR DIGIVICES

An age-old mystical fighting weapon, our Digivices activate when we are in trouble or need extra help!

They are an important part of helping our Digimons Digivolve to higher levels, as Gabumon is doing here!

Thanks to our Digivices, Gabumon Digivolved into his Champion level, the even more powerful Garurumon!

FIGHTING THE

FEAR THE BLACK GEAR

There seems to be an UNLIMITED supply of these Black Gears around, waiting to turn good Digimons into bad ...

BLACK GEARS!

Mojyamon

Just when Matt and Tai thought they were safely through Freeze Land, this big lunk comes along. But Garurumon and Greymon saved the day!

Whamon

Whamon swallowed us all on our way to the Continent of Server! Luckily we got his Black Gear out and he took us to a cool underwater store.

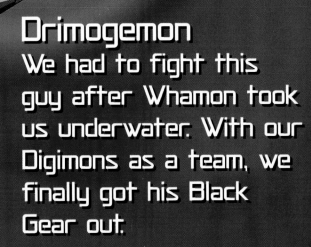

Drimogemon

We had to fight this guy after Whamon took us underwater. With our Digimons as a team, we finally got his Black Gear out.

DIGI-HEAR?

- Black Gears function below the earth, called forth by Devimon, the evil dark force, to do his bidding.

- The more Black Gears inserted in a Digimon, the bigger, stronger, and meaner it becomes.

- Broken Black Gears can fix themselves, and are controlled by Devimon.

- On File Island there is a mountain of Black Gears.

- When Digimons are tired, they have a harder time defeating Black Gears.

- Light from Digivices draws Black Gears out of Digimons.

- Digivices are powerless in the hands of anyone but the Digidestined.

OUR CRESTS:

Matt:
Friendship

T. K.:
Hope

Our crests are like Digivices but even more powerful! They help our Digimons Digivolve to even higher levels than before. Matt found his crest down in a well while he was visiting Piximon!

A DIGI-SECRET MESSAGE*

*To read, hold in front of mirror

With friendship and hope, you can be stronger too!

BIGGEST AND EVER!

We'll never forget the time that evil Kokatorimon turned all our Digimons to stone! We got him back in the end though!

"Matt,
be careful or
the monster
will get you."
— T. K.

BEST BATTLES

"Hey, over here, you overgrown water lizard."
— Matt

Then there was the time Seadramon really looked like he had Matt! But Gabumon attacked and knocked Seadramon on his slimy tail!

T. K. didn't know what he was in for at that amusement park with Devimon. He thought they would find Matt. Devimon had Patamon by the ears before we chased him off!

Patamon always had trouble Digivolving, but he finally does and faces down one of the most evil of all Digimons, Devimon!

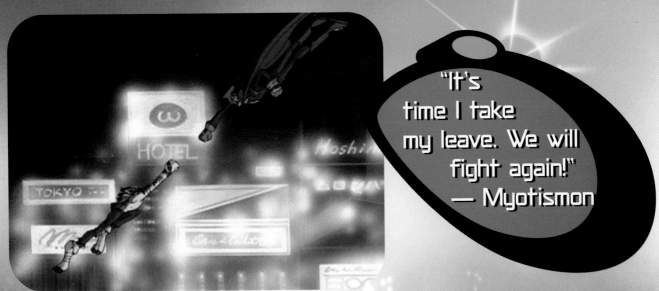

"It's time I take my leave. We will fight again!"
— Myotismon

During one of our trips back through the vortex into the real world, Patamon Digivolved to Angemon to help WereGarurumon fight the unbelievably evil and powerful Myotismon. We got rid of him ... but for how long?

Mojyamon, that bad mountain-like guy in the fur coat, just about had us all right over the edge when Gabumon Digivolved to Garurumon, snatched away Mojyamon's bone, and knocked him over the head with it!

It's amazing what a little Digimon like Patamon can do up against a big guy like Leomon who has a Black Gear stuck in him!

Garurumon really tangled up with Tuskmon in an effort to protect Tai's little sister Kari.

DIGI-SEE?

- Myotismon almost defeated WereGarurumon with his Crimson Lightning!

- When Leomon sends fire from his fist, his face appears in the ball of fire!

- Devimon has the power to split File Island into pieces!

- Patamon beat Elecmon in a tug-of-war!

- Angemon turned into an egg after his first fight with Devimon!

WHAT'S COOL ABOUT

Matt loves playing his harmonica with Gabumon.

DIGIWORLD

Primary Village!

- Where the baby Digis hatch!
- Elecmon, their caretaker, feeds the baby Digis fish!
- Baby Digis hatch out of multicolored eggs!
- Digi eggs can be cracked open by rubbing them gently.
- Baby Digis look like other Digimons at first, then change as they grow up and Digivolve!

T. K. loves just hanging with his best friend Patamon.

WHAT BUGS DIGIWORLD

There's a certain person named Tai who is probably Matt's best friend and also the one thing or person about DigiWorld that drives Matt the most crazy! They just can't agree on anything!

US ABOUT

We also hate ...

- Rotten weather!

- Bad transportation!

Too much crying! Not only does T. K. cry, even his Digimon does it!

THE BAD GUYS

We'll start by separating the children from their parents. Ah, how they'll scream and weep. Delicious."
— Myotismon

After going through the vortex to the real world to fight the evil Digimons that Myotismon let through, we got back to DigiWorld only to find it ruled by a big bunch of even more powerful, more evil Digimons.

"Soon now, not in fire or ice but in fog, this world will be mine." — Myotismon

Myotismon

opens the gate to the real world letting all kinds of new evil in!

Puppetmon

tries to do in all the kids so he can be the evil ruler of DigiWorld!

Cherrymon

tries to talk Matt into fighting Tai!

Phantomon

was sent by Myotismon to round up everyone in the city and hold them hostage!

BROTHERLY LOVE

It sure is nice to have a big brother to run to when you're feeling lost and scared.

When we're all together with our Digimons, Patamon and Gabumon, those are the best times in the world! Too bad that in the real world, we can't live together with our Mom and Dad.

One of our favorite times was when we camped out and ate fish we caught (even if Matt did get a little annoyed).

Matt can still remember when T. K. was a little baby, how he used to take care of him.

Boy, it is just the coolest thing to have your brother by your side to cheer when a battle is won!

"Gabumon, go over and lay down by my brother...your fur is making me sweat."
— Matt

"Thanks, Matt."
— T. K.

GABUMON AND SO COOL!

Gabumon and Patamon take care of us more than we know. Patamon helps T. K. feel safe, and not so scared. Gabumon keeps a cool head when Matt is ready to fly off the handle.

PATAMON ARE

Gabumon and Patamon would do anything for us! One time, when Matt was freezing cold, Gabumon took off his fur and put it on Matt to keep him warm!

Patamon showed T. K. everything there was to know about baby Digis!

Myotismon sent two of his henchmen, Pumpkinmon and Gotsumon, to do damage in the real world, but our Digimons soon convinced them they'd be better off just having a good time! It's hard for these good Digimons not to make friends ... like when T. K. and Patamon visited Primary Village, they got to know all the baby Digis!

Gabumon sure protected Kari, Tai's sister, during one of our stays in the real world.

Gabumon is really a good friend who understands when you just need to go off and have some time and space to yourself.

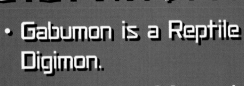

- Gabumon is a Reptile Digimon.
- Patamon is a Mammal Digimon.
- Garurumon, Gabumon's Champion form, is a Mammal Digimon.
- Angemon, Patamon's Champion form, is an Angel Digimon.
- Gabumon's weapon is HOWLING BLASTER.
- When Garurumon Digivolves to his Ultimate form, he becomes WereGarurumon and his weapon is WOLF CLAW.
- WereGarurumon is an Animal Digimon.
- Patamon doesn't Digivolve to Angemon very often because he knows that T. K. needs him in his Mammal Digimon form to comfort him and make him feel secure.
- Gabumon's fur is removable!

GARURUMON RULE!

When Patamon Digivolves to his Champion form, boy does he ever: He becomes Angemon, a mighty Angel Digimon with great power over good and evil. Angemon comes only when he is absolutely, positively urgently needed!

Garurumon's Blue Blaster breath is legendary, but so is his fur. It's as strong as steel. Tentomon once said that Garurumon is "like a growling torpedo."

AND ANGEMON

The first time that Patamon Digivolved into Angemon was to fight Devimon, and he used up so much strength doing it that when the fight was over, Angemon devolved back into a Digi egg.

"Angemon, shall we take him?"
—WereGarurumon

Garurumon Digivolves to WereGarurumon!

Metal Garurumon and War Greymon face down VenomMyotismon!

People in the
real world
couldn't
believe their
eyes when
they saw
these Digimon
Champions!

CAN WE EVER FROM EVIL?

Sometimes it seems like we keep fighting and fighting, and the evil Digimons just get stronger.

SAVE THE EARTH

Myotismon has the crest of the eighth Digidestined child and he seems determined to get her.

He sends some pretty bad monsters into the real world to cause destruction.

Meanwhile, we have to protect Tai's sweet little sister Kari. I sure hope we can save her from the clutches of Myotismon.

WHO KNOWS WHAT WILL HAPPEN NEXT?

Well, as long as we have each other for brothers, we're in this thing together!

DIGI-SECRET
MESSAGE*
*To read, hold in front of mirror

The eighth
Digidestined child is
Tai's sister Kari.